Josephine County Library
Grants Pass, Oregon

In Memory of
KAYE JEAN TURNER

Wolfgang Amadeus Mozart
Musical Genius

Stewart Ross

Chicago, Illinois

Titles in this series:
Muhammad Ali: The Greatest—Neil Armstrong: The First Man on the Moon—Fidel Castro: Leader of Cuba's Revolution—Roald Dahl: The Storyteller—The Dalai Lama: Peacemaker from Tibet—Anne Frank: Voice of Hope—Mahatma Gandhi: The Peaceful Revolutionary—Bill Gates: Computer Legend—Martin Luther King, Jr.: Civil Rights Hero—John Lennon: Musician with a Message—Nelson Mandela: Father of Freedom—Wolfgang Amadeus Mozart: Musical Genius—Florence Nightingale: The Lady of the Lamp—Pope John Paul II: Pope for the People—Pablo Picasso: Master of Modern Art—Elvis Presley: The King of Rock and Roll—Queen Elizabeth II: Monarch of Our Times—The Queen Mother: Grandmother of a Nation—William Shakespeare: Poet and Playwright—Vincent Van Gogh: The Troubled Artist

© 2004 Raintree
Published by Raintree, a division of Reed Elsevier, Inc.
Chicago, Illinois
Customer Service 888-363-4266
Visit our website at www.raintreelibrary.com

For information, address the publisher:
Raintree, 100 N. LaSalle, Suite 1200, Chicago, IL 60602

Library of Congress Cataloging-in-Publication Data
Ross, Stewart.
  Wolfgang Amadeus Mozart / Stewart Ross.
    p. cm. -- (Famous lives)
Summary: Introduces the life and work of composer Wolfgang Amadeus Mozart, whose works include "The Marriage of Figaro," "The Jupiter Symphony," and "The Magic Flute."
Includes bibliographical references (p.   ) and index.
  ISBN 0-7398-6627-3 (library binding-hardcover)
  1. Mozart, Wolfgang Amadeus, 1756-1791--Juvenile literature.
2. Composers--Austria--Biography--Juvenile literature. [1.
Mozart, Wolfgang Amadeus, 1756-1791. 2. Composers.] I.
Title. II. Series: Famous lives
(Chicago, Ill.)
  ML3930.M9R67 2004
  780'.92--dc21

                        2003004013

Printed in Hong Kong

07 06 05 04 03
1 2 3 4 5 6 7 8 9 0

Cover: A portrait of Mozart as a young boy.
Title page: Wolfgang Amadeus Mozart, the Austrian composer in later life.

Picture acknowledgments
The publisher would like to thank the following for permission to reproduce pictures:
pp. 4, 20, 37 Mary Evans Picture Library; pp. 5, 6, 7, 8, 9, 11, 12–13, 14, 15, 17, 18, 19, 21, 23, 24, 25, 26, 27, 28, 29, 30, 31, 32, 33, 34, 35, 36, 39, 40, 41, 43, 44 AKG; pp. 10, 16, 42 Bridgeman Art Library; p. 22 Hodder Wayland Picture Library; p. 38 Sylvia Corday; p. 45 Redferns.

Cover picture: AKG
Title page picture: Mary Evans Picture Library

Note to the Reader
Some words are shown in bold, **like this.** You can find out what they mean by looking in the glossary.

Contents

The Prodigy

The room was very large and very elegant. The many important people seated within it were among the grandest of Vienna, the capital city of the mighty Austrian **Empire.** The flickering light of hundreds of candles glimmered on their priceless jewels.

Yet the attention of everyone within that room, from the count and countess in the front row to the motionless servant by the door, was focused on a small boy.

The focus of a young musician's dreams: the palace of the emperor of Austria in Vienna.

The child genius: Mozart at the age of six. It was common in those days for children to be painted as little adults.

The six-year-old child sat before a **harpsichord.** Like his audience, he wore fancy clothes of high fashion. At a nod from his father, the boy raised his little hands and began to play. His tiny fingers danced over the ivory keys, filling the room with music as sweet as summer honey.

The audience smiled and nodded to each other. Yes, this boy from Salzburg was indeed remarkable: Wolfgang Amadeus Mozart was a true **prodigy.**

Surrounded by Music

Wolfgang Amadeus Mozart was born in the Austrian city of Salzburg on January 27, 1756. Wolfgang's father, Leopold Mozart, was a musician. In 1747 he had married Maria Anna Pertl, a young woman from a respectable middle-class family like his own. They had seven children. Only two—Wolfgang and his elder sister, who was named Maria Anna after her mother but was known as "Nannerl"—survived infancy.

The house in Salzburg in which Wolfgang was born on January 27, 1756. Today it is a museum.

"Moreover, I must inform [you] that on January 27, at 8 P.M., my dear wife was happily delivered of a boy.... Now (God be praised) both child and mother are well." Leopold Mozart writing to a friend on February 9, 1756, about the birth of Wolfgang.

A portrait of Maria Anna, Wolfgang's mother.

We know little about Wolfgang's mother, Maria Anna. She seems to have left her children's upbringing almost entirely in her husband's hands.

Like most Salzburg musicians, Leopold was employed by the **prince-archbishop.** In 1757 he was promoted to court composer. He was a talented violinist and a successful music teacher. His handbook on violin teaching (1756) was translated into several languages. Wolfgang was surrounded by music from the moment of his birth.

"A Miracle"

By Mozart's third birthday, his parents realized he was not
a normal child. He had enormous energy, both mental and
physical, and staggering talents. At four he could draw, solve
math problems, and use words expertly.

Above all, he had an amazing musical instinct. He seemed
to discover music within him rather than learn it. It was as
if he had been born with a musical soul.

*Mozart playing the violin,
accompanied by his sister
and father.*

"God has let a miracle see the light in Salzburg.... And if it ever is to become my duty to convince the world of this miracle, the time is now, when people ridicule and deny all miracles."
Leopold Mozart, writing to Lorenz Hagenauer about his son's talent.

King Joseph introduces his mother, Empress Maria Theresa, to the young Mozart, October 1762. Painted more than 100 years later (1869), the picture is a romantic recreation of the scene.

By age five Mozart was **composing** simple musical pieces. He had learned to play the clavier (an early form of piano) and violin well, but he hated the trumpet. He did not like its harsh sound.

Mozart's father could hardly believe his son's abilities. A man of strong religious faith, he decided such talent must be a gift from God. It was his duty, therefore, to help develop the gift. He also realized that his son's talent would be a welcome source of extra income.

Sensible Advice?

In Mozart's time, Western music was totally different than it is today. Because electricity had not been discovered, music could not be recorded—it could only be heard by people attending a concert in person. Sound could not be amplified with microphones and speakers, nor were there electronic instruments, such as electric guitars.

Many wealthy families held private concert parties where they could experience live music in their own homes.

Joseph "Papa" Haydn (1732–1809), the finest composer in Austria before Mozart. The young Mozart dedicated several pieces to Haydn.

"This piece was learned by Wolfgang on January 24, 1761, three days before his 5th birthday, between 9 and 9:30 in the evening." Leopold Mozart, proudly writing in his daughter Nannerl's music book in 1761.

The law was also very different from today in that it did not protect composers. Anyone could give a public performance of a piece of music or sing a song without paying the composer anything. Composers made money only when someone paid them to write a new piece.

Mozart's father knew about all of these difficulties. He urged his brilliant son to keep in the good graces of the rich—the **prince-archbishop** of Salzburg, for example. However, even when he was young, Mozart found his father's sensible advice hard to follow. He knew he was a genius and was unwilling to act impressed by anyone, however rich.

On the Road

In 1762 Leopold decided to present his son to the world. He traveled to the German city of Munich with Nannerl and Wolfgang. (Germany at that time was several cities and states, not a single country.) Here the children played before the elector (prince) of Bavaria.

From Munich the trio went to Vienna. Although Nannerl, now age eleven, was a fine musician, it was the six-year-old Wolfgang who stole people's attention. His talent even impressed Maria Theresa, the empress of Austria. The travel, concerts, music lessons, and presentations lasted almost four years.

> "Master Mozart ... is but Seven Years of Age, plays anything at first sight, and composes amazingly well. He has had the honor of exhibiting before their Majesties greatly to their satisfaction."
> A comment about Wolfgang's talents in the *Public Advertiser* newspaper, London, May 9, 1764.

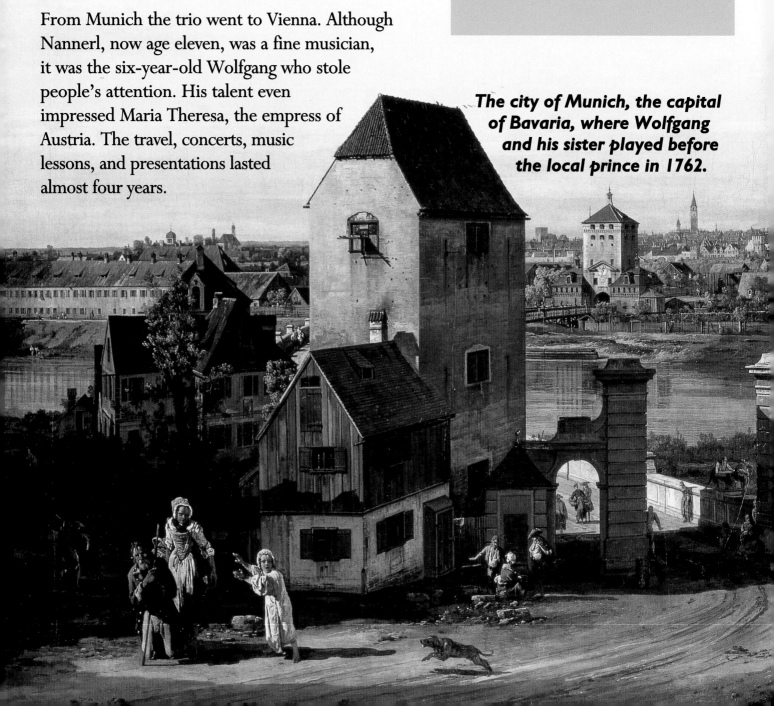

The city of Munich, the capital of Bavaria, where Wolfgang and his sister played before the local prince in 1762.

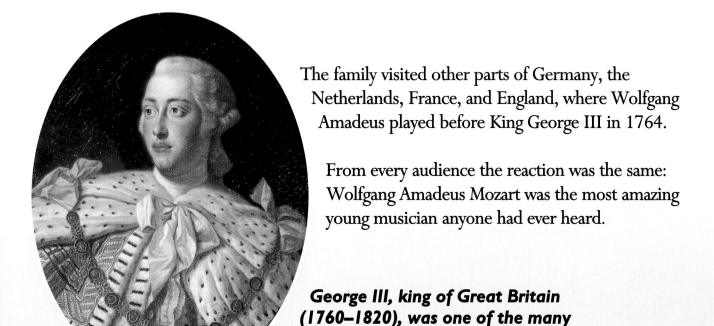

The family visited other parts of Germany, the Netherlands, France, and England, where Wolfgang Amadeus played before King George III in 1764.

From every audience the reaction was the same: Wolfgang Amadeus Mozart was the most amazing young musician anyone had ever heard.

George III, king of Great Britain (1760–1820), was one of the many grand figures who were astonished by the talents of the young Mozart.

Father and Son

Wolfgang Amadeus Mozart's three-and-a-half-year tour of Europe was an unusual education. It was not necessarily a bad one, though. The boy met all kinds of people, especially musicians; saw famous sites; and learned foreign languages.

The devoted, organized Leopold kept up his son's musical education, too. The relationship between Wolfgang and his father has always fascinated scholars. Some blame Leopold for being too harsh on the boy, forcing him to grow up too fast and to be too disciplined about his talent.

Entertaining the French nobility: Wolfgang, seated at the piano, in Paris, 1763.

A young man at the piano, about 1765. The picture is believed to be of Wolfgang at the age of nine.

Others say that someone as high-spirited as Wolfgang needed a steady hand like Leopold's to guide him. Without his father's help, they say, the world might never have seen the genius of Wolfgang Amadeus Mozart.

The Mozart family spent 1767 mainly in Salzburg. Wolfgang and Nannerl both caught smallpox, a deadly disease that often left survivors with scars. Luckily, they recovered, and the next year the twelve-year-old Wolfgang was off on his travels again.

Italy and the Opera

Rome as it was at the time of Mozart.

Mozart spent many of his teenage years in Italy, where he was much loved. At the time Italy, like Germany, was divided into many cities and states. One of the most powerful of these was Rome, ruled by the pope (the leader of the Catholic church). Understandably, it was an important center of religious music. Italy as a whole, however, was most famous for its **opera.**

16

MITRIDATE
RE DI PONTO,

DRAMMA PER MUSICA
DA RAPPRESENTARSI
NEL REGIO-DUCAL TEATRO
DI MILANO
Nel Carnovale dell' Anno 1771.
DEDICATO
A SUA ALTEZZA SERENISSIMA
IL
DUCA DI MODENA,
REGGIO, MIRANDOLA ec. ec.
AMMINISTRATORE,
E CAPITANO GENERALE
DELLA LOMBARDIA AUSTRIACA
ec. ec.

IN MILANO.)(MDCCLXX.

Nella Stamperia di Giovanni Montani.
M.169a CON LICENZA DE' SUPERIORI.

PERSONAGGI.

MITRIDATE, Re di Ponto, e d'altri Regni, amante d'Aspasia.
Sig. Cavaliere Guglielmo D'Ettore Virtuoso di Camera di S. A. S. Elettorale di Baviera.
ASPASIA, promessa sposa di Mitridate, e già dichiarata Regina,
Signora Antonia Bernasconi.
SIFARE, figliuolo di Mitridate, e di Stratonica, amante d'Aspasia,
Sig. Pietro Benedetti, detto Sartorino.
FARNACE, primo figliuolo di Mitridate, amante della medesima,
Sig. Giuseppe Cicognani.
ISMENE, figlia del Re de' Parti, amante di Farnace,
Signora Anna Francesca Varese.
MARZIO, Tribuno Romano, amico di Farnace.
Sig Gaspare Bassano.
ARBATE, Governatore di Ninfea,
Sig. Pietro Muschietti.

Compositore della Musica.

Il Sig. Cavaliere Amadeo Wolfgango Mozart, Accademico Filarmonico di Bologna, e Maestro della Musica di Camera di S. A. Rma il Principe, ed Arcivescovo di Salisburgo.

M.169b   ATTO

A program of one of the first productions of Mozart's opera Mitridate.

Amazingly, while still in his early teens Mozart was already writing operas of his own. One, *Mitridate,* was given 21 performances in Milan in 1770–1701. In the same year he did something else extraordinary. He heard the pope's Sistine Choir sing a work—*Miserere* by Gregorio Allegri—known only to themselves. After listening to the piece, Mozart wrote out the whole thing from memory!

As a young child Mozart had been famous as a performer. He still played, of course, but his chief interest now was in **composing** new music.

The Concertmaster

*Mozart's master:
Hieronymus Colloredo,
the prince-archbishop
of Salzburg.*

In 1773, at the age of 17, Mozart asked to work as a musician at
the court of Empress Maria Theresa in Vienna. He was rejected.
If he had acted more **humble,** he might have succeeded. But
Mozart was not humble and he would not beg.

Small, bright-eyed, and energetic, Mozart said what he thought. He was supremely confident in his own talent. He knew he had a unique ability. More importantly, he wanted to be recognized and to live in the sort of style he felt his talent deserved.

> **"Salzburg is no place for my talent."** Mozart writing to Abbé Bullinger in 1778, realizing that he would never be fulfilled if he stayed in his hometown.

Mozart felt cramped in Salzburg, particularly after the rather narrow-minded Hieronymus Colloredo became **prince-archbishop** in 1772. After working for Colloredo as his *Konzertmeister* (concertmaster), in 1777 Mozart set out with his mother for Paris. There, he was sure, his talent would be fully recognized.

Even before he reached Paris, his plans were upset by something unexpected. While traveling through Mannheim, he fell in love.

The Seine River and the Notre Dame Cathedral in Paris. In 1777 Mozart set out to make his fortune in the city.

Love and Sadness

Mozart had fallen for Aloysia Weber, the pretty 16-year-old daughter of a musician. His mother did not mind the relationship, but his father was furious when he heard of it. His son must concentrate on music alone, he said, and ordered him to proceed to Paris. Mozart, now 21, obediently did as he was told.

First love: Mozart at the piano, accompanying Aloysia Weber.

"I, who from my youth have never been accustomed to look after my own things, linen, clothes, and so forth, cannot think of anything I need more than a wife." Mozart writing to his father, explaining why he needs a wife.

A small orchestra at the time of Mozart.

In Paris the young genius attracted much attention. He earned **commissions** for new music, including a sparkling **concerto** for harp and flute. But he was not offered a high paying job. More tragically, his mother fell ill and died on July 3, 1778.

Now traveling alone, Mozart slowly returned home. His father had arranged for him to be promoted to Colloredo's court organist. Before reaching Salzburg in January 1780, Mozart visited the Weber family. Aloysia, now a successful singer, was not interested in him.

21

"The Kindest Heart in the World"

Mozart was now recognized as the most talented young musician in Germany. It was no surprise when, in 1780, the Prince of Munich **commissioned** him to write a new **opera.** Called *Idomeneo,* it was warmly praised when first performed early the next year.

A manuscript of one of Mozart's early works.

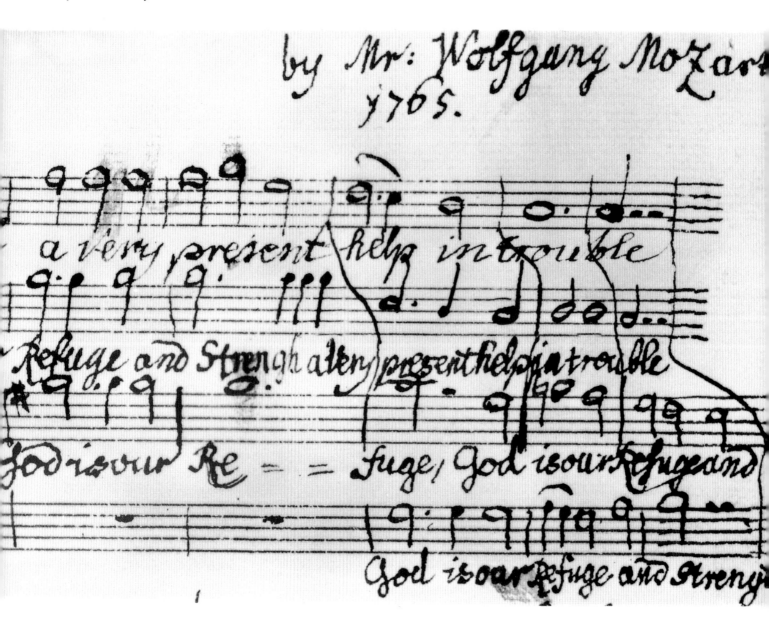

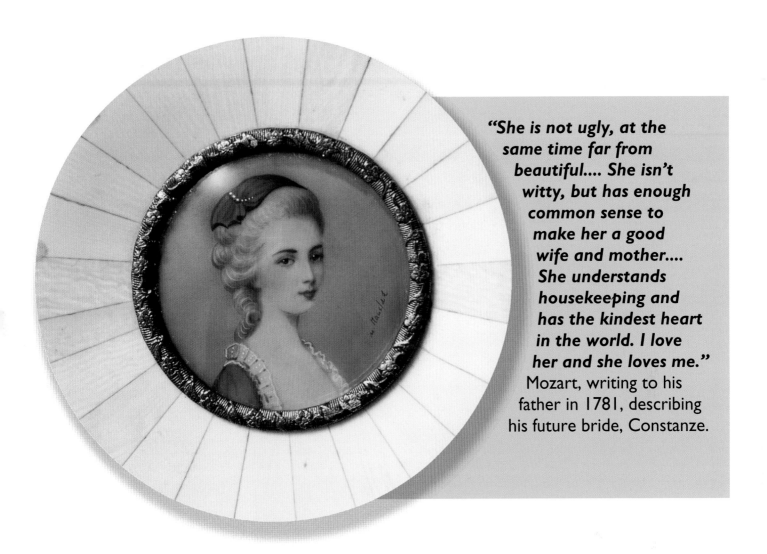

"She is not ugly, at the same time far from beautiful.... She isn't witty, but has enough common sense to make her a good wife and mother.... She understands housekeeping and has the kindest heart in the world. I love her and she loves me." Mozart, writing to his father in 1781, describing his future bride, Constanze.

A miniature painting of Constanze Weber at the time of her engagement to Mozart in 1781.

Fresh from his Munich triumph, Mozart went to Vienna, where **Prince-Archbishop** Colloredo was attending the **coronation** of the new Austrian **emperor**, Joseph II. Annoyed at the way the prince-archbishop treated him, Mozart resigned from his service on June 9, 1781. He was now a free man.

Staying in Vienna with his old friends the Webers, who now lived there, Mozart fell in love again. His new love was Constanze, Aloysia's 18-year-old sister. The couple became engaged at the end of 1781 and were married on August 4, 1782. Although Leopold was not pleased, he could do nothing about it. Mozart had declared his independence.

Unique Talent

Now that we have followed Mozart to the height of his success, it is time to take a closer look at his music. Unlike today, in Mozart's time there was no real separation between serious music, such as **compositions** for a church service or concert, and popular music, or songs that might be sung or played at home. Mozart composed music for dances as happily as he wrote **operas.**

In Mozart's time all music used similar instruments: strings, woodwind, brass, percussion, and keyboards.

Mozart **composed** a wide range of pieces. His work ranged from writing for one single instrument to composing for small groups of musicians to creating large pieces for **ochestras** using many different instruments.

A painting of the apartment that Mozart lived in from 1784 to 1787.

Johann Sebastian Bach (1685-1750), the German composer whose work had a deep influence in the 1700s and beyond.

"Die Entführung aus dem Serail [The Escape from the Seraglio, *an opera***] *appeared here this year; the music for this opera has been made by Herr Mozart.... The author's taste and new ideas, which were entrancing, received the loudest and most general applause.*"** A Hamburg magazine praising Mozart's music in 1783.

Mozart developed his unique music from what he heard. In London he came across the work of Johann Christian Bach, the son of Johann Sebastian Bach, who had been the finest musician of the previous generation. In Italy he picked up the native opera style, and in Paris the French style of writing for an orchestra. In Vienna he learned from Joseph Haydn, the most respected composer of his day.

Mozart's brilliant mind absorbed these influences and mixed them with his own genius to produce some of the most remarkable music ever written.

Family Life

Years after Mozart's death, his wife, Constanze, would remember that he had sometimes flirted with servant girls. Nevertheless, their marriage was a very happy one. Her love for him did not fade and she supported him in all he did. For his part, he went to great lengths to keep his "Stanzerl" (his nickname for Constanze) as happy as possible.

Constanze in 1782. Mozart loved her dearly.

Mozart's children: on the left is Franz Xaver Mozart and on the right, Karl Thomas Mozart.

"Dearest, most beloved friend ... Everything depends, my only friend, upon whether you can and will lend me another 500 gulden." Mozart writes a letter to a friend begging for money in 1789.

Between June 1783 and July 1791 the couple had six children. Not unusually for those days, only two—Karl Thomas (born 1784) and Franz Xaver (born 1791)—survived more than six months. Continual childbearing was hard on Constanze's health. By the 1790s her medical treatments were very expensive.

Husband and wife shared a love of the high life, including fine clothes, servants, and a carriage. Although Mozart earned far more than most other musicians, he also spent more. As a result, although Constanze and he were never poor, they were often short of money.

"The Land of the Piano"

People were amazed by how many different kinds of music Mozart succeeded in **composing.** He excelled in all three branches of serious music: **chamber music** (for a small number of instruments), orchestral music (for the many instruments of an **orchestra**), and vocal music (for voices).

The beautiful clothes of these musicians suggest they may have been performing at a special event like a royal banquet.

A painting of Mozart produced many years after his death.

Vienna—nicknamed "the land of the piano"—loved Mozart, and in the year following his marriage his concerts there were packed. He composed several lively piano **concertos** (for piano accompanied by an orchestra), grand **symphonies,** and delightful string quartets (for two violins, viola, and cello). His opera, *Die Entführung (The Escape from the Seraglio),* was very popular, and his religious music reached new depth and maturity with the **Coronation** Mass.

His only disappointment was his failure to get a job at the court of the **emperor.** This was partly because he was not friendly with the court musicians led by Antonio Salieri.

"It is hardly possible for anyone to stand beside the great Mozart ... It enrages me to think that the unique Mozart has not yet been engaged [hired] by a ... royal court."
Joseph Haydn expressing frustration that Mozart was not able to play for royalty.

"The Greatest"

In 1785 Mozart met the **librettist** (writer) Lorenzo da Ponte. Their partnership produced the glorious **opera** *Le nozze di Figaro (The Marriage of Figaro).* It was first staged in Vienna in 1786 and then in Prague.

A scene from the opera The Marriage of Figaro, which is still performed to packed houses all over the world.

Meanwhile, Joseph Haydn had written to the elderly Leopold Mozart, "Your son is the greatest composer known to me in person." This was praise indeed. Others were even more enthusiastic: Some said he was the greatest composer who ever lived.

30

Mozart recognized his own importance and started to make a catalog of his music. He was also admitted to the Vienna branch of the Freemasons, an exclusive Christian society.

The 29-year-old composer's tragedy was that he had to work unbelievably hard to earn what he felt he deserved. Most other musicians would have been thrilled to have created just one of these works. However, Mozart drove himself, month after month, to produce a stream of outstanding compositions. Sadly, as a result of this hardwork, his health began to suffer.

Another painting of Mozart: titled **Mozart Composing,** *it tries to capture the ease with which brilliant music came to him.*

Court at Last

Mozart's father died on May 28, 1787. Although father and son had been living far apart for years, Mozart was surprised and saddened at the news of his father's death. The man who had created him as a person and a musician was now gone.

There were other family tragedies, too. The previous year his and Constanze's third son had died almost immediately after his birth. In 1787 Constanze gave birth to a daughter who died six months later.

Musically, Mozart continued to excel. His new **opera** with da Ponte, *Don Giovanni*, was a major success in Prague.

The theater in Prague in the 1700s. The city commissioned Mozart's opera Don Giovanni; one of his compositions from the time is known as the Prague Symphony (1786).

Ludwig van Beethoven, the young composer who impressed Mozart when they met in 1787.

"Mozart ... said vivaciously, 'Keep your eyes on him; some day he will give the world something to talk about.'"
Beethoven, age 17, recalls overhearing Mozart predicting his success.

And finally, **Emperor** Joseph II gave him a court position, although a minor one. As composer of music for court balls, he produced one of the most famous pieces of **chamber music** of all time: *Eine kleine Nachtmusik (A Little Night Music).*

"Black Thoughts"

By 1788 Mozart was not as fashionable in Vienna as he had been. Surprisingly, *Don Giovanni,* now considered brilliant, was not a success when produced in the city. As determined as ever, Mozart worked on what proved to be his last and greatest **symphonies:** numbers 39, 40, and 41.

Emperor Joseph II, an excellent musician, once agreed to sit down and play one of Mozart's pieces with him. When they were ready, the emperor was surprised to see that the composer had no music before him. Asked where it was, Mozart pointed to his head. "In there!" Mozart replied with a grin.

"Mozart's music is certainly too difficult for the singers." Emperor Joseph II commenting on the **opera** *Don Giovanni.*

Pictures from an early production of **Don Giovanni.**

Joseph II, the emperor of Austria who failed to find an important court position for Mozart.

Delightful music was not the only thing whirling round Mozart's mind. He was tired and depressed by his constant lack of money, by the deaths of his children, and by Constanze's poor health.

To his dismay, he found "black thoughts" creeping into his exhausted brain.

Debt

Early in 1789 Mozart was cheered up by an invitation to visit the court of the king of Prussia, Frederick William II, who ruled over lands which are today part of Germany. He traveled to Berlin with Count Karl Lichnowsky through Prague, Dresden, and Leipzig. In Berlin he wrote **chamber music** with parts specially written for members of the Prussian royal family.

Count Karl Lichnowsky, the nobleman who helped both Mozart and, later, Ludwig van Beethoven.

Mozart toward the end of his life. In reality he would probably have been much thinner than this.

Back in Vienna, his gloom deepened. Constanze gave birth to another daughter, who died almost immediately. The poor mother's medical bills piled up.

The small salary (800 gulden, or Austrian dollars; about the same as 4,000 American dollars today) from the Austrian court was not enough to support the Mozarts in their accustomed style. To meet their expenses, Mozart borrowed heavily, particularly from his Freemason friend, Thomas Puchberg.

In the fall, as Europe reeled from news of a revolution in France, Mozart began his third **opera** with da Ponte. As with his previous works with the same **librettist,** the **commission** had come from the city of Prague.

A Grim Year

The year 1790 was not a good one for the Mozart household. To begin with, Constanze and Wolfgang were in poor health. She was exhausted by constant childbearing, and he was depressed and bothered by headaches and pains in his joints. Their financial problems did not get any better, either.

His new **opera,** *Così fan tutte,* had only five performances. The show was forced to shut down when Joseph II died and the government closed all theaters as a mark of respect.

The health spa at Baden today. In the late 1700s, Constanze Mozart would have spent many weeks trying to regain her strength at a similar spa in Baden.

Mozart did not give up, however, and saw the **coronation** of a new **emperor** as a fresh opportunity for him. He traveled to various cities in hopes of obtaining new **commissions**. He went to the coronation of Leopold II in Frankfurt in 1790 and put on a concert to attract attention.

However, the composer had not chosen his moment well. The concert was poorly attended, and he lost money and brought himself nothing but more headaches.

*A drawing of the
costume design for a
production of Mozart's
Così fan tutte. When
this opera was first
performed it closed
after only a handful
of performances.*

The Magic Flute

At the turn of the year, things began to improve for Mozart. He was appointed assistant to the elderly *Kapellmeister* (Chapel Master) of St. Stephen's Cathedral in Vienna. There was a good chance he would soon inherit the highly paid post.

A drawing of the original production of Mozart's last and most widely appreciated opera, The Magic Flute.

In the spring an old friend, Emanuel Schikaneder, paid the composer handsomely to write the music for his new **opera,** *Die Zauberflöte (The Magic Flute).* Before it opened, the city of Prague **commissioned** yet another opera—*La clemenza di Tito (The Clemency of Titus)*—to celebrate the **coronation** there of Leopold II.

There were other commissions, too, including one for a clarinet **concerto.** Furthermore, to the delight of both Mozart and his wife, their sixth child, Franz Xaver, was born strong and healthy.

> *"Did I not tell you that I was composing this 'requiem' for myself?"* Mozart speaking about **composing** the requiem on his deathbed.

The strain of all this work took a toll on the composer's health. Moreover, he had also received a strange and somewhat sinister **commission**: an **anonymous** figure was paying him to write a **requiem.** Mozart had uneasy feelings about whom it was for.

A grand design for a 1799 production of Mozart's opera **The Clemency of Titus.**

41

Requiem

Throughout the summer, as he labored on *The Magic Flute* and *The Clemency of Titus,* Mozart felt increasingly unwell. Doctors tried in vain to diagnose the illness. We now believe he suffered from uremia, a kidney disease. It was certainly made worse by lack of rest.

On September 30 he was only just well enough to conduct the first performance of *The Magic Flute.* The show was an instant success. Sadly, though, the composer's life was drawing to a close. He died at 12:55 A.M. on December 5, 1791, at the age of 35. The **requiem,** which had been **commissioned** by a local nobleman for his young wife, remained unfinished.

An artist's impression of Mozart's final hours, spent listening to a rehearsal of his requiem.

Constanze was overcome with grief and climbed into bed beside her dead husband. Later she recovered sufficiently to accompany the corpse to St. Mark's Cemetery. Here, witnessed by only a handful of mourners, the body of one of the world's greatest musical geniuses was laid to rest in an unmarked grave.

"Stay with me tonight; you must see me die. I have long had the taste of death on my tongue, I smell death...." Mozart speaking to his wife, Constanze, as he lay dying.

A painting of the manuscript of Mozart's last work: the requiem.

His Talent Lives On

Constanze recovered from her husband's early death and remarried. For the rest of her life she tried to make people realize Mozart's importance to the world. Even so, the exact place of his grave was forgotten. It was not until 1859 that a marble monument was built near the spot.

"It may be said that untold tears were shed for Mozart; not only in Vienna, perhaps still more in Prague.... Every connoisseur [admirer of fine things] and lover of music considered his loss irreplaceable...."
Franz Xaver Niemetschek speaking about his friend Mozart in 1808.

The monument that marks the approximate resting place of perhaps the most gifted musician who ever lived.

The Mozarts' surviving children did not inherit their father's musical genius. Karl Thomas, a minor government official in Milan, died in 1858. Franz Xaver was a good musician but never became as famous as his father. He died in 1844.

Later in the 20th century, Mozart's reputation soared. By the time the **bicentenary** of his death was celebrated in 1991, many people agreed that the world will probably never see such a genius again.

The performance goes on: a modern production of Mozart's **The Magic Flute.**

Glossary

anonymous created by someone unknown

bicentenary Two-hundredth anniversary

chamber music music for a small group of instruments

commission pay for the creation of a new work of art, such as a piece of music

compose write music

composition a written piece of music

concerto piece of music played by an orchestra and a solo instrument

coronation ceremony in which a crown is placed on a new ruler's head

emperor the ruler of an empire. The emperor in Mozart's time ruled the Holy Roman Empire (around 800 A.D. to 1806), which included parts of what is now Germany and Italy.

empire group of lands governed by an emperor

harpsichord keyboard instrument in which the strings are plucked

humble without pride

librettist writer of lyrics for an opera

opera play in which the words are sung rather than spoken, accompanied by music

orchestra many instruments that play together under the leadership of a conductor

prince-archbishop leader of the Catholic churches in Salzburg during Mozart's time

prodigy someone who shows unusual talent at a very young age

requiem religious service for the soul of someone who has died

symphony large piece of music for an orchestra

Further Information

Books to Read

Brighton, Catherine. *Mozart: Scenes from the Childhood of the Great Composer.* London: Frances Lincoln Limited, 2000.

Isadora, Rachel. *Young Mozart.* New York City: Viking, 1999.

Lynch, Wendy. *Mozart.* Chicago: Heinemann, 2000.

Malam, John. *Wolfgang Amadeus Mozart.* Minneapolis: Carolrhoda Books, 1998.

Salvi, Francesco. *Mozart and Classical Music.* Hauppauge: Barron's Educational Series, 1998.

Date Chart

January 27, 1956 Wolfgang Amadeus Mozart born in Salzburg, Austria

1760 Begins music lessons with his father, Leopold Mozart

1761 Composes his first music

1762 First public performances in Munich and Vienna

1763–1766 Taken by his father on a tour around many countries, including the Netherlands, France, England, and many German states

1764 Writes his first symphony

1767 Writes his first piano concerto

1769–1771 First visit to Italy

1772 Hieronymus Colloredo becomes prince-archbishop of Salzburg.

1777 Leaves for Paris and falls in love with Aloysia Weber

1778 Mother dies in Paris

1779 Becomes court organist in Salzburg

1781 Mozart resigns from position in Colloredo's court. He lives in Vienna, meets Joseph Haydn, and writes the opera *The Escape from the Seraglio*.

1782 Marries Aloysia Weber's sister, Constanze; writes a series of fine piano concertos

1784 Son Karl Thomas born; Mozart joins Freemasons

1785 Begins work with da Ponte on the opera *The Marriage of Figaro;* finishes series of Haydn string quartets

1787 Mozart meets Beethoven. Prague commissions *Don Giovanni.* Mozart's father Leopold dies. Mozart is made a minor court composer for Joseph II, and writes *Eine kleine Nachtmusik.*

1788 Writes his last symphony, no. 41 (later called the "Jupiter")

1789 Mozart visits Berlin. Revolution breaks out in France.

1790 Mozart is frequently ill, but he attends the coronation of Leopold II in Frankfurt.

1791 Son Franz Xaver is born. Mozart writes his last piano concerto, his clarinet concerto, *The Magic Flute* (opera), and his unfinished requiem. He dies on **December 5** at age 35.

Museums and Festivals

There are several Mozart museums in Salzburg, Austria, the town of his birth. Information can be obtained from:

Internationalen Stiftung Mozarteum
Schwarzstraße 26
A-5020 Salzburg, Austria

There is also a Mozart museum in Prague, the Czech Republic.

Each year festivals of Mozart's music are held not just in Austria but all over the world.

Index

All numbers in **bold** refer to pictures as well as text.